THE INTERNATIONAL STUDENTS' GUIDE TO COOKING WITHOUT GETTING CAUGHT is a spectacular book which details how to cook without a kitchen in a student dorm. It breaks no cooking rules since it is done without toasters, broiler ovens and hot plates.

Each recipe takes five to ten minutes of cooking time. They are cheap, innovative and easy.

The Author is a twenty-one year old college student.

The International Students' Guide to Cooking Without Getting Caught

The International Students' Guide to Cooking Without Getting Caught

by

Terry Fisher

ASHLEY BOOKS, INC.
Port Washington, New York 11050

Published simultaneously in Canada by
George J. McLeod, Limited, 73 Bathurst Street,
Toronto, Ontario M5V 2P8

THE INTERNATIONAL STUDENTS' GUIDE TO COOKING
WITHOUT GETTING CAUGHT
© Copyright 1976 by Terry Fisher
Library of Congress Number: 76-18503
ISBN: 0-87949-055-1

Address information to Ashley Books, Inc.
Box 768, Port Washington, New York 11050

Published by Ashley Books, Inc.
Manufactured in the United States of America

First Edition

9 8 7 6 5 4 3 2 1

CONTENTS

INTRODUCTION — Dear Reader.............................11

BREAKFAST..17
Boiled Eggs...19
Fancy Baked Eggs...20
Creamed Eggs on English Muffins.........................22
Cheese Omelet..23
Grilled English Muffins...................................24
Instant Oatmeal & Cream of Wheat.......................25
Seasoned Grits..26
Granola Oatmeal..27

LUNCH AND DINNER......................................29
How to Cook Pasta and Rice...........................31
Creamy Noodles..34
Casseroles..37
　　　American Chop Suey................................39
　　　Tuna Newburg Casserole...........................40
　　　Cheesy Casserole...................................41
　　　"Anything Goes" Casserole.........................42
　　　Pizza Casserole....................................43
Hot Pot Specials..45
　　　How to Cook Fresh Vegetables......................47
　　　Corn Pudding.......................................48
　　　Eggplant Parmesan..................................49
　　　Beef and Vegetable Bake............................50
　　　Chili with Beans....................................51
　　　Meat Loaf...52
　　　Hot Dog Quiche.....................................53
　　　Always Fails Cheese Souffle.........................54
　　　Sloppy Joes...55

Ironing It Out...57
    Steak Sizzle..59
    Fish Sticks...60
    Ten-Minute Mini Pizza.................................61
    Pot Pies..62
    Golden Cheese Presses.................................64

EASY EMBELLISHMENTS...................................65
Low-Cal Dip..67
Pea Soup...68
Macaroni Salad...69
Super-Soft Rolls...70
Instant Gravy..71
Thick Cheese Sauce...73
Low-Cal Salad Dressing.....................................74

LET THERE BE BREADS!.....................................75

SWEET THINGS..81
Upside-Down Pudding Cake...................................83
Fudge Cake Float...84
Bread Pudding..85
Crustless Pumpkin Pie......................................86
Fruit Crunch...87
Apple Betty..88
Caramel Apple Bake...89
Fruit Pudding..90
Caramel..91
Cinchy Fudge...92
Instant Chocolate Fondue...................................93
Rice Krispie Bars..94
Peanut Butter Chews..95
Protein-Rich Cheesecake....................................96
Homemade Pineapple Jam.....................................97

AUTHOR'S NOTE...99

The International Students' Guide to Cooking Without Getting Caught

Dear Reader:

Do you love to cook, but have no kitchen to cook in? Or maybe you hate to cook and have neither the time nor desire to spend more than five or ten minutes to prepare a meal. Either way, this book is written for you.

When I first came to the University of Virginia two years ago, I was in both these situations at once. I lived in a dorm without any kitchen; for our meals we had several options—buying a meal ticket, eating out every day, or finding something that didn't need cooking. And then there was the time element; often I had so much studying that I didn't have the time to take fifteen minutes to walk to the cafeteria, wait in line for half an hour (sometimes even an hour), eat, and then walk back again. Besides, I wasn't thrilled with the food and I knew I could eat cheaper on my own. After the first semester I refunded my meal ticket.

Our dorms had very strict cooking rules. We were not allowed to have hot plates, toasters, or portable broiler ovens. We were allowed to have hot pots (which boil water) but we could only use them for coffee or tea. (Later we were allowed popcorn poppers, but only for popcorn.) Of course, most of us stretched that rule and we boiled water for instant oatmeal, Cup-a-Soup, and boiled eggs. Quite soon, I became tired of these meals (Who wouldn't?), but since I was trying to save money, I refused to spend it eating out. I decided, then, to find a few more uses for my hot pot. One of my first attempts was bread pudding. I had to use powdered eggs and dry milk, since I didn't have a refrigerator then. (We were allowed to have small refrigerators, and at the end of the

11

year I bought a used one for thirty dollars. It was the best thirty-dollar investment I ever made.)

I also found that macaroni would cook in a thermos filled with boiling water, and I could wrap cheese sandwiches in aluminum foil and "grill" them by ironing them. It became a challenge to see what I could make without resorting to the traditional method of using an oven and stove. This book is the result of those experiments that were successes.

Now, to illustrate my simple cooking appliances. This is a hot pot:

Its main purpose is to boil water, though some hot pots come with a filtering device to use for perking coffee. It is cheaper ($4-$6) to get one without the filter; you won't use it for anything here, anyway. **Important:** Make sure it's the type that will continuously boil water—some of the more expensive ones automatically adjust to a lower temperature once the water has started to boil. The hot pot can be used to make a complete meal—soup, casseroles, and dessert.

This is an old iron:

It had been used to iron clothes until I got hold of it. Now it fries steaks for me, while my poor clothes remain somewhat ignored. Notice that it doesn't have any steam holes; that's because the non-steam type is cheaper. Don't worry, though, if you have a steamer; it will work just as well. You will be wise to use an old iron which you no longer use to iron clothes. Even a steak well wrapped in aluminum foil can leak onto your iron and ultimately ruin your clothes. If you don't have an old iron, look in a thrift shop. You can probably buy a used one there for very little.

This is a thermos:

A pint is a good size to have. Only the breakable glass kind is acceptable because it is the only kind that really is able to keep foods hot. This clever gadget will cook macaroni and oatmeal for you without wasting electricity —remember the energy crisis?

You'll also need some "pots" and "pans." For example, a small pyrex dish with a cover is great if you can find one. It should be able to sit on top of your hot pot like this:

13

It's especially useful for macaroni casseroles. But nothing beats disposable pots—tin cans—and disposable frying pans—aluminum foil (which doubles as a lid). Also, use a small wooden board to iron on so that you don't burn your desk or countertop. Add a measuring cup and some silverware and you'll be ready to get the final "utensil"—food.

Maybe you are still skeptical about what could possibly be cooked without an oven or stove. Well, flip through the pages and see for yourself. Don't be surprised when you see goodies, like fudge, omelets, split pea soup, and even pizza. None of these are difficult, and although the cooking time may be an hour or more, the actual work that you do will only be about ten minutes.

You will need to learn a few new cooking techniques, such as how to preheat a thermos, and how to remove a can from your hot pot without getting a steam burn. To preheat a thermos, simply fill it with hot water, cap it, and let it stand a few minutes. Pour out the hot water just before putting in the ingredients. To remove a can from the hot pot, the trick is to pour cold water over the can and into your hot pot, and to grab the can before it gets hot again. If you merely use a potholder, a steam burn is inevitable.

You will also need a new attitude for most of these recipes—don't worry about timing. A casserole can cook half an hour longer than it needs and still be just as good, and a loaf of bread can steam all day without being any worse for it. But in iron-cooking, the object is the same as ironing—don't burn it. In trying to keep these recipes easy, I have limited the ingredients so that very few recipes have more than five. For example, I often use pudding mix to act as both a sweetener and a flavoring, and cream style Cup-a-Soup is invaluable because it and boiling water are the only ingredients needed to make a creamy, well-seasoned sauce for casseroles.

Since I realize low-calorie recipes are always welcome, I have tried not to add any unnecessary calories. You will notice that very few of these recipes have any short-ening which can add calories so easily. Some recipes are made especially for dieters, such as the cheesecake, salad dressing, and dip. On the other hand, the fudge and caramel are definite no-no's if you are trying to diet. They are so good it is impossible to take "just a taste."

I have divided this book into three parts: breakfast, main meal, and desserts. The first section has instruc-tions for cooking eggs and grilling English muffins. The second part includes recipes for main dishes, like Tuna Newburg Casserole, Eggplant Parmesan, chili, and meat loaf, as well as directions for cooking prepared frozen foods, like pot pies, pizza, and fish sticks. The last section has recipes for desserts, snacks, and sweets. I've included treats like puddings, breads, Rice Krispy Bars, and candy.

Almost all the recipes are made to serve one person. This is mostly because a hot pot or thermos is really too small to make a large amount, also because I don't think you'll have the occasion to serve a crowd from your hot pot. If you do have to feed more than two people, give up this method and find a real kitchen!

Love,

Terry

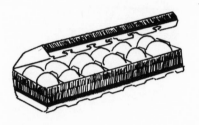

Breakfast

I think that everyone will agree that
breakfast should be quick and easy to make—
at least, when I get up, I'm not in the mood to
make a gourmet meal. But it should be worth
getting up for, right?
Read on!

Boiled Eggs

Eggs are the most classic American breakfast, and boiled eggs are the easiest.

Put the eggs in your hot pot and cover them with cold water, then plug the hot pot in. Don't put the eggs directly into boiling water as they might crack. They will be hard-boiled fifteen minutes after the water begins to boil. For soft-boiled eggs, reduce the cooking time to suit your taste.

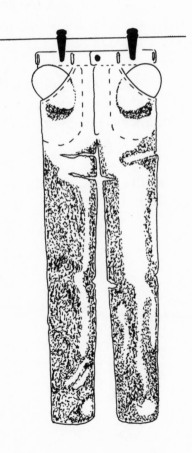

Fancy Baked Eggs

If you're feeling more ambitious some morning, try these eggs which are "baked" in a creamy sauce. They taste fattening, but there are only 125 calories in a serving.

3 Tbsp. boiling water
2 Tbsp. cream-of-chicken Cup-a-Soup mix
1 egg

You will need a small aluminum pie tin (the size used for individual pot pies). Mix the water and soup in the tin. Carefully break the egg *onto* this sauce—the object here is *not* to drown the egg. Cover the tin with aluminum foil. Then put this on top of your hot pot, which has boiling water in it. Let the egg steam this way for about twenty minutes for a well-cooked egg, or less for a softer egg.

Variation: Sprinkle the egg with grated cheese or bacon bits before you cook it.

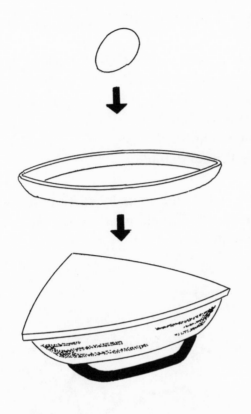

1 Egg   =   1 Omelet

Pie Tin   =   Frying Pan

Iron   =   Stove

Creamed Eggs on English Muffins

Here is another fancy but easy breakfast treat.

2 Tbsp. cream-of-chicken Cup-a-Soup mix
¼ cup boiling water
1 chopped hard-boiled egg
1 "grilled" English muffin

Stir the water and soup together until there are no lumps, then add the chopped egg. Pour this over the English muffin.

Cheese Omelet

Turn your iron into a stove for this one and use an aluminum pie tin for a frying pan. Your arm may get a little tired, but it's worth it.

1 egg
1 Tbsp. milk
½ Tbsp. butter
1 oz. shredded cheese

Preheat your iron to the highest setting. Beat the egg and milk together. Then hold your iron upside down so that you can use the flat part for a "stove." Put the butter into an 8″ aluminum pie tin (the bottom of the tin will be only about 6″). Then place it on top of your "stove," and wait until the butter has melted and is sizzling. Pour in the egg mixture and let it cook for about four minutes, or until the egg is almost set. (You will have to turn the pie tin so that all the egg can get done evenly, since an iron isn't wide enough for the whole pie tin.) Then sprinkle the cheese over it and cook it for another minute. Remove it from the iron. Fold the omelet over so that the cheese is inside, and serve.

Variations:
1) Add some chopped ham or drained mushrooms with the cheese.
2) Add 1 tsp. sugar to the egg mixture and cook it until it's set, omitting the cheese. Spread with jelly or jam before folding.

"Grilled" English Muffins

Better than toast any day.

Split and butter an English muffin. Put the two halves side by side on a piece of aluminum foil and wrap the foil over them. "Grill" your muffins by ironing both sides with a medium-hot iron until they're toasted to perfection.

Instant Oatmeal and Cream of Wheat

You can buy instant oatmeal and cream of wheat which have already been sweetened and flavored, but I think it's more fun to create my own flavors. Simply add 1 or 2 Tbsp. of dry pudding mix to a packet of instant cereal and add boiling water to make it the right consistency. You'll love chocolate oatmeal with lots of cream!

Seasoned Grits

Instant grits come flavored with ham or bacon, but you can season plain grits by adding 1 or 2 Tbsp. of cream-of-chicken Cup-a-Soup mix, or make cheese-flavored grits by adding grated cheese. If you prefer sweetened grits, add 1 or 2 Tbsp. of dry pudding mix.

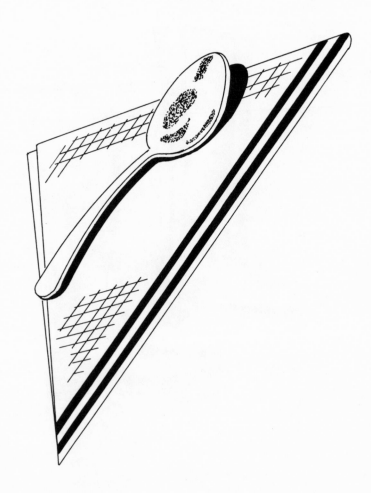

Granola Oatmeal

This is my favorite hot cereal. It has the flavor of granola, the texture contrasts of nuts and raisins, and the warmth of a hot cereal. You can make it before you go to bed, and it'll be ready for you in the morning, or earlier, if you can't wait that long. You'll need a preheated thermos for this.

  ½ cup granola with fruit and nuts
  ¾ cup boiling water

Put the granola and boiling water into the thermos, close it, and shake it for a few seconds. The cereal will be cooked in about two hours, but it can sit indefinitely and still stay hot.

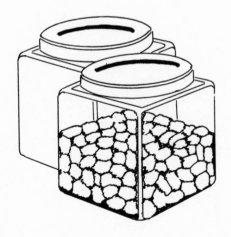

Lunch and Dinner

This section concentrates on lunch and dinner menus. There are many recipes for casseroles which can be cooked in a can inside your hot pot or in a dish on top. I was lucky enough to find a small pyrex dish with a cover, and the dish fits perfectly on my hot pot without wobbling. However, if you can't find a small pyrex dish, a pot-pie tin will work, although it won't be able to hold as much. You can cook the casserole in a can, but use rice instead of macaroni or noodles — it'll give better results.

There are also recipes for chili, Sloppy Joes, and instructions for cooking steak, pizza, and other goodies. All these are made with only three utensils: a hot pot, an iron and a thermos!

How to Cook Pasta

There are two ways you can cook macaroni and noodles—either in a thermos or in a pyrex dish on top of your hot pot. The first method has the advantage of saving electricity, but I have included the second method in case you don't have a thermos.

Method 1

Put about 1/3 cup of macaroni shells or twists (not elbows—they tend to stick together) into a preheated thermos. Add at least 1 cup of boiling water and a dash of salt. Close the thermos and shake it for a few seconds. In about thirty to forty-five minutes the macaroni will be done. To cook noodles, use about 2/3 cup of noodles. Drain off any remaining water.

Method 2

Put about 1/3 cup of macaroni, or 2/3 cup of noodles, into a small pyrex dish. Add one cup of boiling water and a dash of salt. Cover the dish and put it over your hot pot, which should have boiling water in it. Let macaroni or noodles cook for forty-five minutes. Drain off any water.

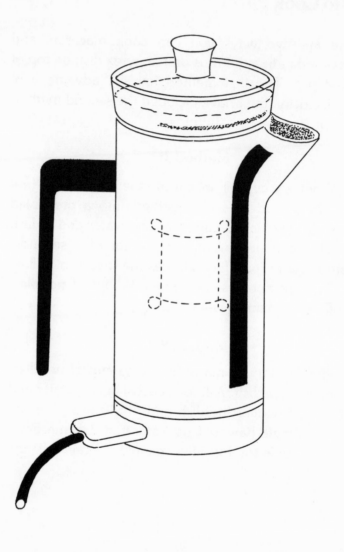

Sitting comfortably in a steam bath

Rice

Put ¼ cup brown rice in a can. Stir in ¾ cup boiling water and a dash of salt. Cover the can with foil and place in your hot pot, filled half way with boiling water, to steam for one hour, or until all the liquid is absorbed and the rice is tender.

Variations:

1) Add 1 tsp. instant bouillon or a bouillon cube to the boiling water and let it dissolve before adding it to the rice. Omit the salt.
2) If you want a firmer rice, use only ½ cup of boiling water.

Creamy Noodles

Let your thermos cook this for you. It's a great way to bring a hot lunch to work—just make it in your thermos in the morning and it'll be ready for lunch whenever you are. Try not to make it too much ahead of time, though, because the noodles will get mushy.

> 2/3 cup noodles (about 1 1/2 oz.)
> 1 cup boiling water
> 1 envelope cream-of-chicken, mushroom, or lobster
>   bisque Cup-a-Soup

Preheat your thermos with hot water, then pour it out.

Put the noodles, soup, and boiling water in a pre-heated thermos, close it, and shake it for a few seconds. It will be done in an hour.

Variations:

1) Add 1 oz. shredded cheddar or American cheese.
2) Add 1 tsp. instant chicken bouillon or one bouillon cube with the cream-of-chicken soup for more flavor.
3) Use 1/3 cup macaroni instead of noodles. After ten minutes, shake the thermos again; otherwise the macaroni will stick together.

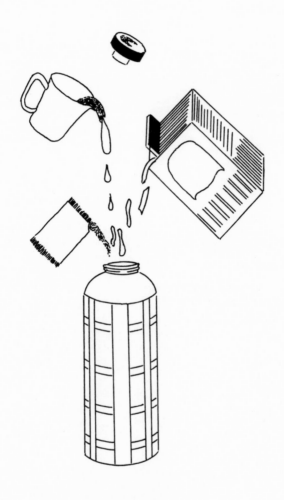

Simply Simple

Casseroles

The next section has casseroles which are cinchy to put together and impossible to burn. However, since different kinds of pasta cook faster than others, the cooking times I have suggested are only approximate. You can tell when a casserole is done if most of the liquid is absorbed and the sauce is thick. Just remember to add water to your hot pot as the water evaporates.

American Chop Suey

⅓ cup macaroni (1½ oz.)
2-3 oz. lean ground beef, crumbled
½ cup canned stewed tomatoes
¼ cup boiling water

Chop the tomatoes, but don't drain them. Add the other ingredients and put them in a small pyrex dish and cover it. Put the dish on your hot pot which should have boiling water in it, and let it steam for 1½ hours. Stir it once or twice while it's cooking.

Variation:

Use ¼ cup brown rice instead of the macaroni, and increase the boiling water to ⅓ cup. Put it in a can, cover with foil, and place it in your hot pot to steam. It'll only take one hour this way.

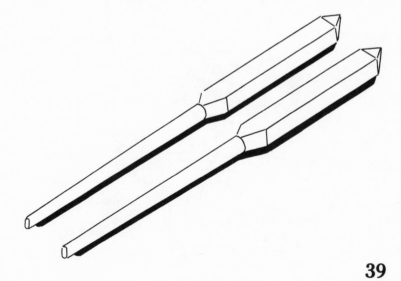

Tuna Newburg Casserole

1 envelope lobster bisque Cup-a-Soup
1 cup boiling water
⅓ cup macaroni or ⅔ cup noodles (1½ oz.)
¼ cup tuna

Mix the water and Cup-a-Soup in a small pyrex dish. Stir in the pasta and tuna. Cover and place on your hot pot to steam for 1½ hours. Stir it once or twice while it's cooking and before serving.

Variations:

1) Use ¼ cup brown rice instead of the macaroni or noodles. Place everything in a can, cover with foil, and put it in your hot pot to steam for one hour. Stir it once or twice.
2) Use any other cream style Cup-a-Soup.

Cheesy Casserole

If you like Swiss cheese, don't miss this. The cheese gets "stretchy" as it melts.

> 1 envelope cream-of-chicken Cup-a-Soup
> 1/4 cup brown rice
> 1 cup boiling water
> 1/4 cup diced ham (optional)
> 1 oz. shredded Swiss cheese

Mix the soup, rice, water and ham in a can, cover with foil, and place in your hot pot to steam for one hour. Then stir in the cheese. Wait until it melts (which will be almost immediately) before serving.

Variation:
Use Mozzarella instead of Swiss cheese. This will stretch indefinitely when you try to eat it. That's the fun of it!

"Anything Goes" Casserole

You can actually look forward to leftovers with this recipe! Even if you don't have any leftovers, I'm sure you'll find something in your refrigerator—or a friend's—to put into this dish.

> 1 envelope any cream style Cup-a-Soup, or ⅓ cup condensed cream soup
> ¾ cup boiling water
> ¼ cup brown rice
> ⅓ cup any diced vegetable or a mixture, raw or cooked
> ¼ cup diced cooked beef, chicken, ham or tuna

Stir the water and soup together in a can, then add the other ingredients. Cover the can with aluminum foil and put it in your hot pot with boiling water for one hour. Stir it once or twice while it's cooking and before serving.

Pizza Casserole

¼ cup canned pizza or spaghetti sauce
⅓ cup macaroni (1½ oz.)
⅔ cup boiling water
2-3 oz. lean ground beef, crumbled
1 oz. shredded Mozarella cheese
2 tsp. grated Parmesan cheese

Mix everything except the cheese in a small pyrex dish. Cover and place on your hot pot to steam for 50 minutes. Stir it, then top with the cheese and let it steam for another 10 minutes or until the cheese melts.

Hot Pot Specials

*These recipes concentrate on the hot pot.
They take some cooking time, but are
well worth the waiting. You can do other
things while the water boils around the
tin can that holds your dinner, and end up
doing two things at once.
Who wouldn't wait for Eggplant Parmesan
or Hot Dog Quiche?*

How to Cook Fresh Vegetables

It's very easy to cook fresh vegetables or potatoes. Simply wash them well, dice them into one inch cubes, and put them in a can which has 2 Tbsp. of water with a dash of salt. Cover the can and place it in your hot pot to steam, until the vegetables are just tender. This will be about thirty minutes to one hour for most vegetables. Season them with salt and butter, or lemon juice, or any way you prefer. Or you may want to top them with a cheese sauce.

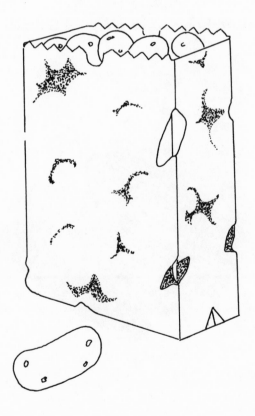

Corn Pudding

Recipes for corn pudding usually use milk, but I like to use cream-of-chicken soup, instead. It gives a richer texture, and, I think, a better flavor.

3/4 cup corn
1 egg
1/3 cup condensed cream-of-chicken soup

Beat the egg and soup together in a can, then stir in the corn. Cover the can with foil and place in your hot pot to steam for forty-five minutes.

Variation: Add one oz. of shredded Swiss or cheddar cheese.

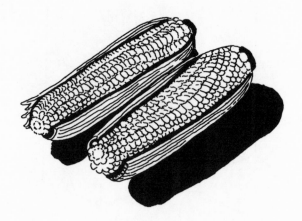

Eggplant Parmesan

Real Eggplant Parmesan is fried first, which adds calories. I don't use any shortening in this recipe, so there are only about 200 calories in a serving. And it tastes just as good!

> 1 cup eggplant, diced
> 1/3 cup canned spaghetti sauce
> 1 oz. shredded Mozzarella cheese
> 1 Tbsp. grated Parmesan cheese

Layer one third of the eggplant, sauce, and cheese in a can. Repeat these layers two more times. Cover the can with foil and put it in a hot pot of boiling water for one hour.

Beef and Vegetable Bake

This has chunks of beef, potatoes and carrots— similar to a stew—and the sauce is rich and creamy.

> 1 envelope cream-of-chicken or mushroom Cup-a-Soup
> ½ cup boiling water
> 3 oz. lean beef, cut into ½" cubes
> 1 small potato, peeled and diced
> 1 carrot, diced

Mix the water and soup in a can. Add the other ingredients. Cover the can with foil and place in your hot pot with boiling water. Forget it for an hour, then stir it once before serving.

Chili with Beans

This will warm you up fast on a cold day!

  3-4 oz. lean ground beef, crumbled
  1 cup drained kidney beans
  ¼ cup undiluted tomato soup
  ½ tsp. chili powder

Stir everything together in a can and cover with
aluminum foil. Put it in a hot pot with boiling water and
let it cook for one hour. You can also put everything in a
covered pyrex dish to steam on top of your hot pot. Stir it
before serving.

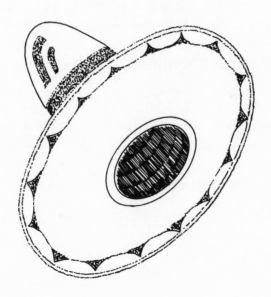

Meat Loaf

Add as many or as few spices as you like. This will serve about three people for one meal, or you can use the leftovers for cold sandwiches.

> ¼ cup boiling water
> ½ envelope cream-of-chicken or mushroom Cup-a-Soup
> 1 slice bread, crumbled
> 1 egg
> 3 Tbsp. chopped onion (optional)
> 1 Tbsp. Worcestershire Sauce (optional)
> 1 tsp. salt
> ¾ lb. lean ground beef

Mix the first three ingredients together well and then stir in the remainder. Place in a pound-size can and cover with aluminum foil. Place in a hot pot with boiling water so that the water almost reaches the top of the can. Let it boil for one hour. Drain off any fat before serving.

Variations:
1) Add 2 Tbsp. ketchup to the meat mixture.
2) Use ¼ cup condensed tomato or cream-of-mushroom soup instead of the Cup-a-Soup and water.
3) Use ½ cup crushed seasoned croutons in place of the bread.

Hot Dog Quiche

Hot dogs and cream-of-chicken soup are used instead of ham and cream as in Quiche Lorraine, but the Swiss cheese is still there. I think you'll like this novel combination, and you won't even miss the pie crust.

1 hot dog, sliced
1 oz. shredded Swiss cheese
1 egg
⅓ cup condensed cream-of-chicken soup

Put the hot dog slices in a pot-pie tin. Top with the cheese. Cover the dish with foil and place it on top of your hot pot to steam for one hour or until the custard is firm. You can also put this in a can, cover it with foil, and place it in your hot pot to steam. This will only take half an hour, but you'll lose the "pie" effect.

Always Fails Cheese Souffle

This "souffle" will fall almost immediately and it won't brown, but it still tastes fine. After all, you can't expect miracles from a little hot pot!

1½ slices bread, cubed
1 oz. shredded cheese
1 egg
½ cup milk

Layer the bread and cheese in a can, beginning and ending with bread. Beat the milk and egg together and pour over the bread and cheese. Let it sit for at least half an hour. Then cover the can and put it in your hot pot to steam for half an hour.

Variations:

1) Substitute ¼ cup of milk with ¼ cup undiluted cream-of-chicken or mushroom soup.

2) Add some diced cooked ham, chicken, egg or tuna with the cheese.

Sloppy Joes

These have a tangy barbecue flavor. Try them open-faced on grilled English muffins for a new way of eating this old favorite.

> 3-4 oz. ground beef, crumbled
> 2 Tbsp. bottled barbecue sauce

Stir the beef and barbecue sauce together in a can. Cover the can with foil and place in your hot pot to cook for half an hour.

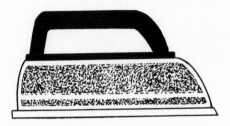

Ironing It Out

The recipes in this section need closer watching—these can burn, unlike the previous recipes. However, they need no preparation, which makes up for the slightly tricky timing element. Here you'll find favorites like steak and pizza. All you need is your hot pot and iron. Remember to find an old iron to cook with, since it might get ruined from those good, juicy steaks that you'll make with it.

Steak Sizzle

When:
1) You crave a steak,
2) You can afford it, and
3) You don't have a stove—
Don't despair!

Use a steak which is only about ¾ inch thick. Sprinkle both sides with salt and then wrap the steak in aluminum foil. With your iron set at medium, iron each side until it looks done on the outside; then cut into the steak to make sure it's done the way you like it. If not, iron it longer.

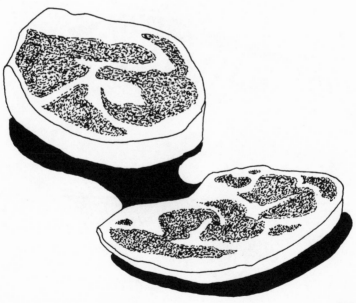

Fish Sticks

Fish sticks can be cooked using the method for steak. Use the precooked-and-frozen type, but let them thaw first, or they'll still be cold on the inside when the outside is done. Preheat your iron to a medium setting. Wrap the fish sticks in aluminum foil and iron each side for about four minutes, or until the crust is golden brown. Frozen crab cakes can also be cooked this way.

These fish sticks are delicious on hamburger rolls with sliced tomatoes, lettuce, cheese and tartar sauce. If you're too broke to afford these luxuries, they are fine with just some ketchup.

Ten-Minute Mini Pizza

Using your hot pot and an iron you can have the individual-size pizzas which come frozen, ready-to-bake. Place a pizza on a piece of lightly greased aluminum foil and put it on top of your hot pot to steam for about five minutes—until the cheese is melted. Meanwhile, preheat your iron to medium—around "wool" is good. Then, holding the iron so that the flat side is up, put the pizza with the aluminum foil on it for five minutes, or until the bottom crust is lightly browned.

Pot Pies

Frozen pot pies can also be "baked" using a steam-and-iron method. Let the pie thaw before you begin; this will shorten the cooking time. Cover the top crust with aluminum foil and set it in the top of your hot pot to steam for forty-five minutes. Preheat your iron to medium. Then, holding the hot side up, put your pot pie on it for five minutes to make the bottom crust crisp. When your arm gets tired, you'll know that five minutes are up! Then put the pie down on a board or heatproof pad, and place the iron on top of the pie to brown the top crust. This will take about five minutes. When you remove the aluminum foil, you'll find a pot pie that looks and smells good enough to eat! Beware though—it's hot!

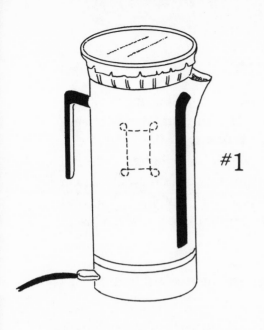

#1

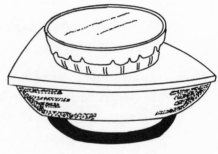

#2

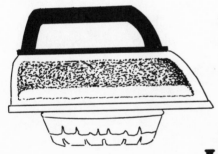

#3

How to make a pot pie in three easy steps.

Golden Cheese Presses

These are an ironed version of grilled cheese sandwiches. Simply place 1 or 2 slices of your favorite cheese between 2 pieces of bread. If you can afford it (calorie-wise, that is) spread the outside with butter—this will make the difference between a good sandwich and a superb sandwich. Then wrap it in aluminum foil and "press" both sides with a medium-hot iron until the bread is toasted and the cheese is melted.

If you want some variety, try these novel and not-so-novel combinations:

1) Peanut butter with cheddar cheese.
2) Sliced bananas with Mozzarella cheese.
3) Ham with Swiss cheese.
4) Tuna or egg salad with American cheese.
5) Bacon and sliced tomatoes with onion-flavored cheese.

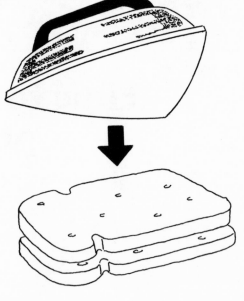

Easy Embellishments

Here I'd like to offer a few odds and ends
which can be used to add variety to a dish or
meal. Some need cooking, some do not.
Adding one of these to a main dish can give
you a multi-course meal for those moments
when you're famished; or you can
use them individually for a quick pick-up.

Low-Cal Dip

There are only about 150 calories for this whole recipe.

½ cup low-fat cottage cheese
2 Tbsp. cream-of-chicken or lobster bisque Cup-a-Soup

Beat the cottage cheese until it's smooth, then stir in the soup mix. Use for vegetables (not crackers—they're too fattening!).

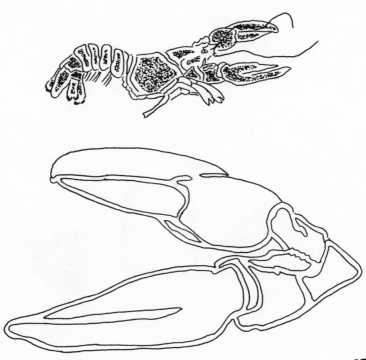

Pea Soup

This is real home made soup, but there's no fuss with seasonings or ham bones. The trick is instant chicken bouillon which seasons the soup perfectly without any chicken flavor.

   ⅓ cup dried split peas
   1 cup boiling water
   1 sliced hot dog
   1 sliced carrot (optional)
   1 tsp. instant chicken bouillon, or 1 bouillon cube

Mix everything in a can, cover with foil, and place in your hot pot to steam for at least two hours—the longer the better. Before serving, stir it well to make a creamy thick soup.

Macaroni Salad

This is a good hot-weather meal, and it can be made ahead of time.

    1 cup cooked macaroni
    ¼ cup diced cooked ham, chicken, egg or tuna
    2 Tbsp. chopped celery
    1-2 Tbsp. mayonnaise

Mix everything together and chill.

Super-Soft Rolls

Wrap some brown paper around a roll and place this on top of your hot pot to steam for a few minutes. The roll should then be very soft, but not soggy. Then steam the other side until it is soft. You might want to split the roll first and slip in a slice of cheese. The cheese will melt while the roll is heating. This is also a very good way to revive stale bread.

Instant Gravy

1 envelope cream-of-chicken or mushroom Cup-a-
  Soup
⅓-½ cup boiling water

Mix ⅓ cup water and the soup until you have a
smooth sauce. Add a little more water if you want it
thinner. Pour the chicken gravy over an open-faced
chicken sandwich or mix with vegetables, diced cooked
chicken, or macaroni for a creamed dish. Use the
mushroom flavor for potatoes or meat.

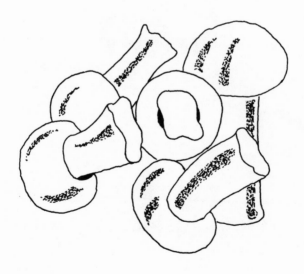

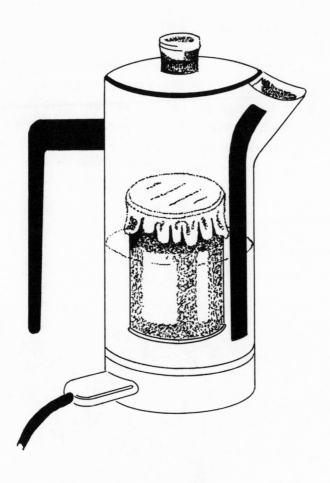

A look inside. . .

Thick Cheese Sauce

Use this sauce to mix with cooked macaroni for macaroni and cheese, to top vegetables or potatoes, or to pour over crackers for rarebit.

    2 oz. diced cheddar or American cheese
    3 Tbsp. milk

Put the cheese and milk in a can, cover it, and place it in your hot pot for thirty minutes, or until the cheese has melted. Then stir the milk and cheese until it's a smooth sauce.

73

Low-Cal Salad Dressing

This salad dressing is thick and rich—not at all watery. You can make any flavor that comes in ready-to-mix packets. Most kinds have only 10 calories per table-spoon. French Riviera, which is my favorite, has 20 calories per tablespoon. You'll need your thermos to make this.

¾ cup boiling water
2 Tbsp. cornstarch
2 Tbsp. cool water
1 envelope dry salad dressing
¼ cup vinegar

Mix the cornstarch with the cool water. Put the boiling water and cornstarch paste into a preheated thermos, close it, and shake it well. Let it sit for fifteen minutes, then pour it into a covered jar and refrigerate until it's cold. Add the vinegar and salad dressing mix and shake it until everything is well mixed.

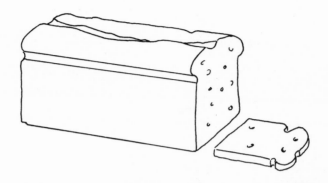

Let There Be Breads!

All the bread recipes on the following pages are prepared by using these basic directions:
Stir all the ingredients together and put into a 16-oz. can. Cover the can with aluminum foil and put it into your hot pot with boiling water to steam for an hour. Don't forget to add more water as it boils away, and don't worry about burning — it will come out the same whether you cook it for one hour or five. I've tried it.

Oatmeal or Bran Bread

⅓ cup biscuit mix
¼ cup oatmeal or bran
¼ cup water
2 Tbsp. brown sugar, honey or molasses
1 Tbsp. raisins (optional)

Orange Bread

½ cup biscuit mix
¼ cup water
2 Tbsp. orange marmalade

Lemon Bread

½ cup biscuit mix
¼ cup water
2 Tbsp. lemon pudding mix

Corn Bread

⅓ cup biscuit mix
¼ cup cornmeal
2 Tbsp. sugar or honey
⅓ cup water

Boston Brown Bread

$1/3$ cup biscuit mix
3 Tbsp. cornmeal
2 Tbsp. molasses
$1/3$ cup water

Pumpkin Bread

$1/2$ cup biscuit mix
3 Tbsp. pumpkin
2 Tbsp. sugar
2 Tbsp. water
$1/4$ tsp. cinnamon

Banana Nut Bread

$1/2$ cup biscuit mix
2 Tbsp. water
3 Tbsp. mashed banana
2 Tbsp. sugar or honey
2 Tbsp. chopped nuts

Peanut Butter Bread

$1/2$ cup biscuit mix
2 Tbsp. brown sugar
2 Tbsp. peanut butter
$1/4$ cup water

Blueberry Bread

½ cup biscuit mix
2 Tbsp. sugar
2 Tbsp. blueberries
¼ cup water

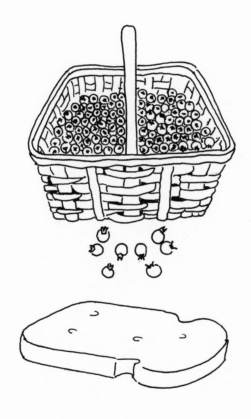

Sweet Things

*Here you will find all kinds of desserts,
sweets, and snacks. There's cheesecake, a
fudge float, Fruit Crunch and caramel. Some
may sound unfamiliar; that's the best reason
to try them. Use your ingenuity to create
your own variations. For example, when a
recipe calls for vanilla pudding mix, be daring
and try a different flavor — maybe coconut
or butterscotch, or try a fruit other than the one
I've suggested. Creating, except for eating,
is the best part of cooking, and it's almost
impossible to fail with these simple recipes.*

Upside-Down Pudding Cake

There is a moist cake on top of a rich caramel sauce in this dessert, which is "baked" in a can. I like to use butterscotch pudding mix because it goes well with the caramel sauce, but any flavor will work just as well.

3 Tbsp. biscuit mix
2 Tbsp. pudding mix
2 Tbsp. water
2 Tbsp. brown sugar
1/4 cup boiling water

Mix the first three ingredients in a can. Sprinkle the brown sugar over the batter and pour the boiling water on top. Cover the can with foil and place it in your hot pot to steam for one hour. Serve it with the sauce on top with ice cream or whipped cream.

Fudge Cake Float

This is another upside down pudding cake recipe. It has chocolate cake floating on lots of thick, hot-fudge sauce. With vanilla ice cream it's like a hot-fudge sundae.

   3 Tbsp. biscuit mix
   2 Tbsp. chocolate pudding mix
   2 Tbsp. water
   2 Tbsp. brown sugar
   1 tsp. cocoa
   ¼ cup boiling water

Mix the first three ingredients in a can. Then sprinkle the batter with the brown sugar and cocoa. Pour the boiling water over all. Cover with aluminum foil and place in your hot pot to steam for one hour.

Bread Pudding

I had never had bread pudding before I tried to make it in a hot pot, and I worried because it was watery, even though it tasted delicious. I was happy to hear from some bread pudding lovers that it's supposed to be that way.

    1 slice bread, cut into cubes
    1 Tbsp. raisins (optional)
    1 egg
    ½ cup milk
    2 Tbsp. pudding mix

Put the bread cubes and raisins into a can. Beat the egg, milk, and pudding together and pour it over the bread. Let the bread absorb the liquid for at least half an hour, then cover the can with aluminum foil and steam it in your hot pot for half an hour.

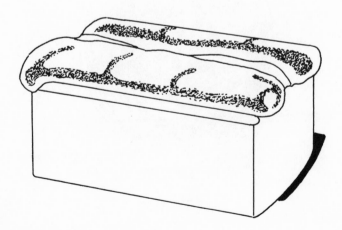

Crustless Pumpkin Pie

Top this with whipped cream and you'll never miss the crust.

 ½ cup canned pumpkin
 ⅓ cup milk
 3 Tbsp. sugar or vanilla pudding mix
 ¼-½ tsp. cinnamon
 1 egg

Mix everything together, pour into a can, and cover the can with aluminum foil. Steam it in your hot pot for thirty minutes.

Fruit Crunch

This is similar to apple crisp, but the crunchy, candy-like topping is on the bottom and in the middle, too—the more the better! You can use either honey or sweetened condensed milk, but I like the condensed milk much better. It gives a rich caramel flavor that honey just can't match.

   ⅓ cup granola
   2 Tbsp. honey or sweetened condensed milk
   1 cup chopped apple or drained canned fruit

Put one third of the granola in a can, top with one third of the honey or condensed milk, and then half of the fruit. Repeat these layers, finally ending with the rest of granola and condensed milk. Cover the can with foil and put it in your hot pot to steam for one hour.

Apple Betty

1 large apple, peeled, cored and diced
1 Tbsp. cinnamon sugar
4 graham cracker squares, crushed
2 Tbsp. water

Put one third of the graham crackers in a can, top with half the apples, and sprinkle with half the sugar mixture. Repeat these layers, ending with the rest of the graham crackers. Pour the water on top. Cover the can with foil and place in your hot pot to steam for one hour. Serve with ice cream or whipped cream.

Variation: Substitute one cup of any canned, drained fruit for the apples; use 2 Tbsp. of the fruit syrup instead of the water. Omit the cinnamon sugar.

Caramel Apple Bake

Do you like caramel apples? Do you like baked apples? Then—

    1 cup chopped apples
    3 Tbsp. sweetened condensed milk

Simply mix the apples and condensed milk in a can, cover with foil, and steam in your hot pot for two hours. It will take this long to become caramelized.

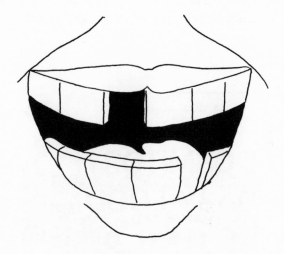

Fruit Pudding

This is thick and sweet like pudding, but pureed fruit is used instead of milk. Baby food is the most convenient fruit to use, but you can make your own by putting fresh or canned fruit in a blender. Give yourself about three minutes to make this.

> 3/4 cup applesauce or other fruit sauce
> 2 Tbsp. instant vanilla pudding
> Cinnamon (optional)

Stir the fruit and pudding mix together until it is very smooth. Add cinnamon to taste, if you wish.

Variations:
1) Use canned pumpkin with 3 Tbsp. of pudding mix and 1/4 teaspoon of cinnamon.
2) Use instant lemon, butterscotch or coconut pudding mix.

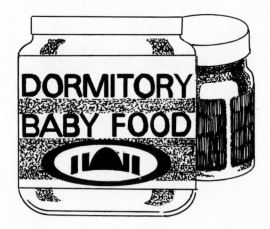

Caramel

I dare any candy store to try to surpass this caramel! It's just the right consistency to spread on apples, but it's also great on ice cream or as a sweet spread for English muffins. This is all you do:

Pour sweetened condensed milk into a can so that it's about half full, then cover the can with foil. Put the can in your hot pot with boiling water and let it boil for about three hours (or longer, if you want). The water level should be higher than the milk level, so remember to add water as it boils away. I guarantee that this will be the best caramel you've ever eaten, and the easiest to make, too. (I used to make this by immersing an unopened can of sweetened condensed milk in boiling water for three or four hours. However, I don't recommend this method, since there is the chance that the can will explode.)

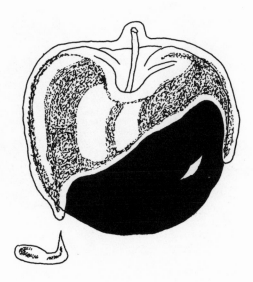

Cinchy Fudge

This fudge needs no boiling or beating—you can't go wrong.

    1 6-oz. package chocolate chips
    ½ cup sweetened condensed milk
    ¼ cup chopped nuts (optional)

Put the chocolate chips in a can and put the can in your hot pot with boiling water in it. Let the chocolate chips melt, stirring them once or twice. Then stir the melted chocolate and condensed milk together until they are completely blended. Add the nuts. Spread the fudge on a greased plate to a thickness of one inch. Chill until firm.

Instant Chocolate Fondue

Here's another dessert for frustrated dieters. (In other words—it's fattening!) The girls I live with at school invented it, and it's so good I can't omit it. But I can't take the credit.

> 1 envelope instant cocoa mix
> 1 Tbsp. boiling water

Stir the cocoa and water together to make a smooth sauce. Add more water if you want it thinner. Use it as a dip for marshmallows, bananas, vanilla wafers or spoonfuls of peanut butter (this tastes like peanut butter cups). I'm sure you'll be able to think of other good "dippers." I bet you'll double or triple the recipe next time.

Variations:
1) Use it as a hot-fudge topping for ice cream or pudding.

93

Rice Krispie Bars

Here are those famous Rice Krispie treats made with marshmallows. They are gooey, but good.

> 2 cups miniature marshmallows or
> 　　20 large marshmallows or
> 　　1 cup marshmallow creme
> 2 Tbsp. butter
> 2½ cups Rice Krispies

Put marshmallows and butter in a can, cover with aluminum foil, and place it in your hot pot to steam for half an hour. Then stir it until it is very smooth. You may have to steam it longer if the marshmallows aren't melted enough. Then add this to the cereal and stir it together well. Spread the mixture about an inch and a half thick on a piece of greased aluminum foil. Cool and cut.

Variations:
1) Add some crushed peppermint stick or other hard candy (about 2 Tbsp.)
2) Use 3 Tbsp. peanut butter instead of butter.

Peanut Butter Chews

This candy-like confection is full of protein and quick energy. They're easy to make, so have them ready to satisfy any "junk food" cravings. Your taste buds will never know the difference.

   ¼ cup peanut butter
   ¼ cup dry milk
   ⅓ cup oatmeal
   ¼ cup instant pudding mix, any flavor
   ¼ cup water

Mix everything together and shape into small balls. Roll them in more oatmeal or confectioner's sugar. Keep refrigerated.

Protein-Rich Cheesecake

Each half cup serving of this cheesecake filling has 15 grams of protein and only 200 calories. It's so rich you wouldn't guess that it has no cream cheese. I like it topped with cherry pie filling, but you can pour it into a graham cracker crust if you want a traditional cheesecake. Don't blink, or you may miss the recipe.

> ½ cup low-fat cottage cheese
> 1 Tbsp. instant vanilla pudding mix
> 1 Tbsp. instant lemon pudding mix

Whir the cottage cheese in a blender or whip it with a beater until it's smooth. Stir in the pudding mix. That's all!

Variations:
1) Use 2 Tbsp. of any flavor instant pudding mix.
2) For a lighter cheesecake, stir in ½ cup whipped topping for each ½ cup cottage cheese that you use.

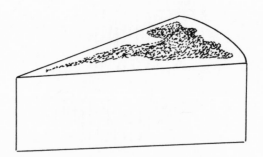

Homemade Pineapple Jam

Here is another quickie using instant pudding mix. This jam has only half the calories of the regular kind.

1 cup juice-packed crushed pineapple
1 package instant vanilla pudding mix

Combine the pineapple and pudding mix until it is completely free of lumps.

AUTHOR'S NOTE

I was born in Cambridge, Mass. on April 24, 1955. I lived in Arlington, Mass. for a short while, but spent most of my pre-school years in Lexington, Mass. Then we moved to Nashua, N.H., where my home is now. I attended grades one through twelve in Nashua, although I spent the summer after my junior year at St. Paul's Advanced Studies Program in Concord, N.H. I graduated second in a class of over 600 students from Nashua Senior High School in 1973.

I am presently a student at the University of Virginia in Charlottesville. This fall will be my third year. I am a Biology major and also pre-med. I intend to be a general practitioner, but if I do specialize, it will probably be in nutrition. I have a particular interest in nutrition because from the tenth grade until just this year I had Anorexia Nervosa. This is a syndrome where dieting becomes an obsession and the person does not stop dieting even though she has become much too thin. I am only 5'1" but I went from 120 lbs. to 75 lbs. Now that I have finally come up to my normal weight I can appreciate how important it is to eat properly and not too much or too little.

I spent this summer at the University of Wisconsin, Madison. I took one course in nutrition and worked part time as a waitress. Although I liked Madison, I will be glad to get "home" to Virginia.

My past jobs have been lifeguarding, waitressing, wait-ressing, and more waitressing. I have done volunteer work at Legal Aid and tutored math when I was in high school. I like to bowl (my average went from 60 to 100 this summer when I joined a bowling league), swim, and dance—especially ballet. I am trying to learn to play tennis and guitar. And, of course, I love to cook and bake. My favorite TV show is Medical Center and my favorite food is ice cream—one of the few things I have not been able to make with a hot pot!

I wrote this cookbook at the University of Virginia as an independent course. Ever since I started college I have been experimenting with cooking in my hot pot. My friends jokingly said I should write a cookbook. So I did. I found a sponsor for this project, but my "find and peck" typing ability was a definite handicap. So we made an agreement—he would type for me, and I would babysit for him. It took me all semester to repay my debt, but it was worth it! The hardest part was to find objective tasters. My suitemates at school gladly tested things for me. I think their opinions, however, were slightly biased since they were always dieting and anything tasted good to them. Jane was the only one who was not dieting, but then, she liked everything, anyway. My sister would have been an objective taster except that she would not go near anything that was made in a hot pot. It turned out that my brother was the most valuable tester. He *said* everything was good, but if he ate something a second time, without my begging, then I knew that recipe had passed. The only problem was that I was not home enough to test many recipes on him. C'est la vie!

Terry Fisher